LET'S THINK AB

the Power of Advertising

Elizabeth Raum

raintree

Raintree is an imprint of Capstone Global Library Limited, a company incorporated in England and Wales having its registered office at 7 Pilgrim Street, London, EC4V 6LB – Registered company number: 6695582

www.raintreepublishers.co.uk
myorders@raintreepublishers.co.uk

Edited by John Paul Wilkins, Clare Lewis, and Kathryn Clay
Designed by Tim Bond and Peggie Carley
Picture research by Liz Alexander and Tracy Cummins
Production by Victoria Fitzgerald
Originated by Capstone Global Library Ltd
Printed and bound in China by CTPS

ISBN 978 1 406 28262 7 (hardback)
18 17 16 15 14
10 9 8 7 6 5 4 3 2 1

ISBN 978 1 406 28267 2 (paperback)
19 18 17 16 15
10 9 8 7 6 5 4 3 2 1

British Library Cataloguing in Publication Data
A full catalogue record for this book is available from the British Library.

Acknowledgements
We would like to thank the following for permission to reproduce photographs:
Advertising Archives: 20, 22; Alamy: © ABN IMAGES, 8, © Asia Images Group Pte Ltd, 26, © BirchTree, 28, © Jeff Morgan_07, 25, © jeremy sutton-hibbert, 32, © Richard Wareham Fotografie, 19, © Todd Bannor, 33, © Wavebreak Media ltd, 27, © Zoonar GmbH, 13, © ZUMA Press, Inc., 34, 35; Corbis: © Bettmann, 14, © Swim Ink 2, LLC, 24; Dreamstime: © Americanspirit, 7; Getty images: Chris Ratcliffe/Bloomberg, 30, 31, kristian sekulic, 29, Mark Davis, 17, ranplett, 6, Robert D. Barnes, 41, Tetra Images, 38; Photo Researchers: 12; Shutterstock: Burlingham, 21 bottom, Gwoeii, 36, HomeStudio, 18, Monkey Business Images, 11, PKOM, 5, Sean Pavone, front cover, tehcheesiong, 21 top; Superstock: euroluftbild.de / F1 ONLINE, 43.

Every effort has been made to contact copyright holders of material reproduced in this book. Any omissions will be rectified in subsequent printings if notice is given to the publisher.

All the Internet addresses (URLs) given in this book were valid at the time of going to press. However, due to the dynamic nature of the Internet, some addresses may have changed, or sites may have changed or ceased to exist since publication. While the author and publisher regret any inconvenience this may cause readers, no responsibility for any such changes can be accepted by either the author or the publisher.

Contents

Some words are shown in bold, **like this.**
You can find out what they mean by looking in the glossary.

We are surrounded by advertisements. Adverts are plastered on buildings and buses. Adverts appear in magazines and newspapers. Adverts play on radio, TV and at the cinema. Huge billboards on the sides of roads advertise services and products to people passing by. Companies often print their names or **logos** on clothing and sports equipment. Sometimes T-shirts feature cartoon or film characters. That's a kind of advertising, too. It draws attention to a particular TV show or film. Many websites carry advertisements. So do video games.

In this book, you'll explore the power of advertising. What is advertising? How does it work? Everyone seems to agree that we are surrounded by adverts. Who creates them and how do they do it? Do adverts change our behaviour? If so, how?

Different views

Many people believe that advertising helps shoppers make good choices. Advertising creates jobs and helps businesses grow. Others claim that advertising causes more harm than good. It encourages people to buy more than they need. It adds to problems of waste and overspending. Some studies suggest that advertising is particularly harmful to children.

What do you think? Once you gather the facts, you'll be ready to form your own opinions and enter the debate.

DID YOU KNOW?

Design student Carolyn Davidson designed the now-famous Nike swoosh logo in 1971. She was paid £21 ($35) for her design.

Buildings in the Tokyo business district are covered in advertisements.

5

What is advertising?

Have you ever made a poster to tell people about a special event? If so, you were advertising. Advertising is a kind of communication. Its purpose is to inform people about a particular event, idea or product. Most advertising is designed to sell products and services. However, businesses are not the only ones who use advertisements.

Political adverts

Politicians use advertisements to present their views and ideas. Political adverts appear on TV, in newspapers and magazines and online. At election time, political advertising increases. Politicians use badges, banners, posters and signs to convince people to elect them to office. Politicians use advertising to reach voters in many different ways.

Signs and posters are a simple kind of advertisement.

Adverts like this try to convince people to change their habits.

Advertising for a cause

Many organizations and **charities** use public service adverts. These adverts tell people about certain causes, provide helpful information or ask for donations. Adverts like the one above try to convince people to change their behaviour and stop smoking. Some public service adverts encourage people to recycle, feed the hungry and drive safely.

DID YOU KNOW?

In 1952 Dwight D. Eisenhower became the first US presidential candidate to advertise on TV. His 30-second adverts appeared during popular American TV programmes. He spent $2 million (£1.2 million) on the adverts. This equals about $18 million (more than £10 million) today. In 2012 US President Barack Obama spent about $100 million (£60 million) on TV adverts. Australia is considering banning political adverts on TV because of the high costs. The UK, like many European countries, limits political advertising.

Selling a product

Most advertisements are designed to sell a product or service. Long ago people depended on friends or family members to tell them about new products. This kind of advertising – word-of-mouth or unpaid advertising – is powerful. We trust friends and family to give us good advice. If a friend tells you something is terrific, you are more likely to try it.

Companies want people to spread good news about their products. But they cannot depend on word of mouth, so they use many kinds of paid advertising. Newspaper and magazine adverts are called print adverts. At one time, print adverts were the most common kind of advertising. Today companies spend more money on TV adverts. They also advertise on the radio, in cinemas and online.

Ambient adverts

Billboards, signs in shops or on streets and adverts on public buses are called **ambient adverts**. Ambient adverts, like the one below, are designed to catch your attention. They are often unexpected and get people talking about the adverts and the product or service it offers. You'll find ambient adverts in unusual places such as on clothing, receipts, pavements or even at the bottoms of swimming pools.

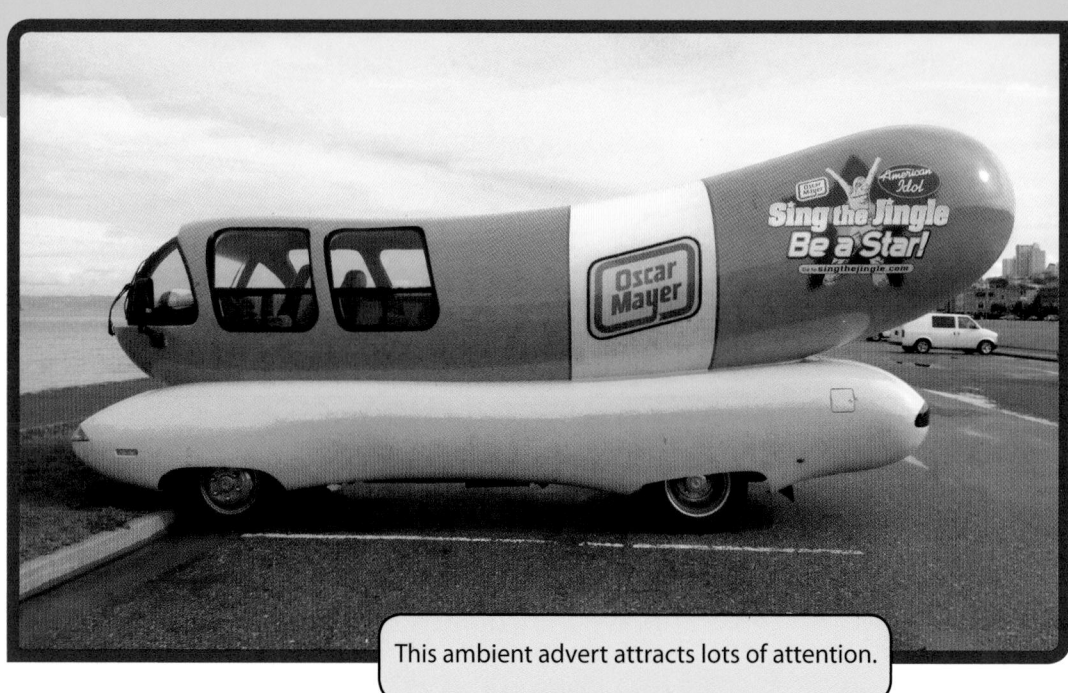

This ambient advert attracts lots of attention.

Total Money Spent on Advertising in 2012

Money (in billions)

US Japan China Germany UK Brazil Australia France Canada Republic of Korea*

Country

*Also called South Korea

Money Spent on Advertising Per Person

Dollars Spent

Australia US Japan Canada UK Germany Republic of Korea* France Brazil China

Country

*Also called South Korea

DID YOU KNOW?

In 2012 companies in the United States spent three times as much money on advertising as any other country. Australia spent the most on adverts per person. China spent the least on adverts per person. However, the amount of money Chinese companies spend on advertising is increasing more rapidly than any other country.

Online adverts

More and more people depend on **digital devices**. So adverts now appear on websites, mobile phones and video games. Many email and social networking sites (such as Google, Yahoo, Facebook and Twitter) keep track of the websites that people visit. This allows them to send **targeted adverts** directly to users' accounts. For example, if you visit websites about bike racing, you might find ads for racing bikes when you log into your email. If you search for information about new cars, new car adverts may pop up when you go online.

Types of Advertising Today

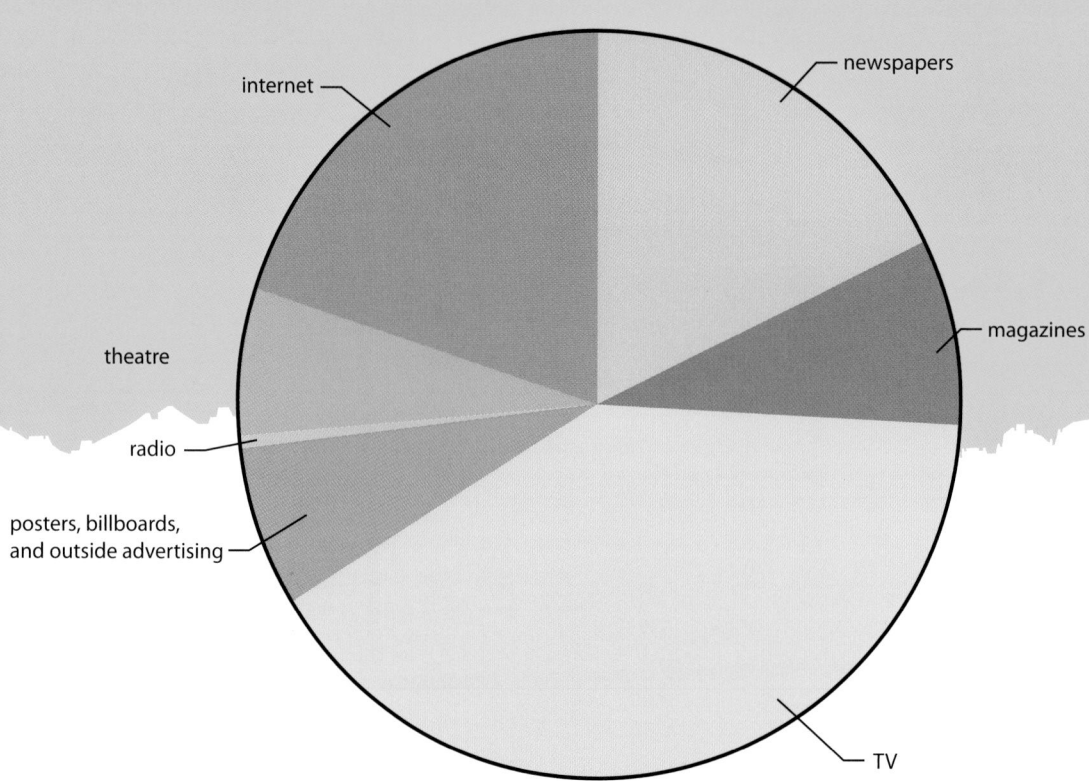

*Information is provided by the AA/WARC Expenditure Report, 2012

In-game advertising appears in the middle of some video games.

Product placement

Even video games have adverts. Sometimes these ads are banners across the top or side of the screen. At other times the adverts are hidden. Perhaps a character is drinking a certain **brand** of fizzy drink or eating at a fast food restaurant. This is called product placement. Product placements are also used in films and TV shows. When film or TV characters wear specific brands of clothes, use brand-name sporting equipment or carry specific kinds of computers or mobile phones, that is product placement. The advertisers make sure the brand names are easy to see.

WHAT DO YOU THINK?

Do you think that advertisers should be allowed to include their products in TV shows, movies and video games? The next time you watch a TV show or movie, look for specific product placements. Keep track of how many you see.

11

In the past people grew their own food, built their own houses and sewed their own clothes. They rarely travelled far from home. However, as the population grew and cities developed, people began depending on others for products and services.

Capitalism

In Europe, the UK and the United States, privately owned businesses provide goods and services. Businesses hire workers, purchase raw materials and turn those materials into new products. Businesses pay their workers, and the workers can then use the money they earn to buy whatever they need or want. This system is called **capitalism**.

In the past shops stocked only a few goods.

Under capitalism each person decides what to buy. People make decisions based on income, prices and their likes and dislikes. This means that businesses must compete for customers. If businesses don't sell their products, they will fail. However, the more they sell, the bigger they will become. Advertising helps businesses make their products known and compete for customers.

WHAT DO YOU THINK?

A modern supermarket carries about 40,000 items. Even simple foods such as bread and milk come in different sizes and flavours. Some people think that life would be simpler with fewer choices. Others say that choices allow us to pick the products that are right for us. Think of a product, such as cereal, that offers many choices. What are the advantages of having choices? What are the disadvantages?

Today shops offer hundreds of choices.

Understanding needs versus wants

In a capitalist system each person makes decisions about what to buy. There are some things that everyone needs, such as nutritious food and warm clothing. There are other things we may want but can live without. These items are called wants or luxuries. Advertising appeals to both our need for basic items and our desire for luxuries.

DID YOU KNOW?

US advertising executive Gary Dahl made millions by convincing people to buy pet rocks. He began selling them in 1975. By the time the fad ended in 1976, Dahl had sold 1.5 million pet rocks for $4 (£2) each. Pet rocks are clearly a want.

	Examples of Needs	Examples of Wants
Drink	water	soda
Food	vegetables and fruits	cookies
Shelter	house or apartment	mansion or castle
Clothing	warm jacket	designer jeans
Activities	playing outside with friends; taking a walk	going snowboarding; going to the movies

The chart above gives clear choices. But sometimes our choices are more complicated. For example, is a bicycle a need or a want? A simple bike that you can ride to school may be a basic need for transport. An expensive racing bike may be something you want. It is important to know the difference. Understanding the difference between needs and wants helps us make good decisions about what we purchase.

WHAT DO YOU THINK?

Make a list of things you want. Put a tick by those that are needs. Look at the ones that are wants. Why do you want them? Is your "want" reasonable? Why or why not?

Helping us decide what to buy

Companies hire advertising agencies to create adverts and put them out to the public. Marketing experts, artists, writers, photographers and salespeople work in advertising. So do computer experts. An advertising agency usually develops an **advertising campaign** for a company. A campaign may include several different kinds of adverts.

This simple model is one way advertisers decide what kinds of adverts to create:

What?	Says what?	To whom?	In what media?	For what purpose?
What product or service does the company want to advertise?	What do they want to say about their product?	Whom are they trying to reach?	Will they use TV, print, online or other media?	What is the hoped-for effect of the advert?
For example:				
ABC Ice Cream Bars	"Everybody loves ABC Ice Cream Bars."	children	TV	Children will want ABC Ice Cream Bars.

Advertising agencies must learn about the company and the company's potential clients. What message do they want to send? What is the best way to send that message? What is their purpose?

Got milk?

In the US, the "got milk?" adverts were named one of the top 10 advertising campaigns of all time. They feature celebrities ranging from Superman to Taylor Swift. Each celebrity wears a milk moustache. The words "got milk?" appear below the picture. The adverts were designed to convince people to choose milk over juice or fizzy drinks. In a 2002 survey, 41 percent of Americans asked said they liked the adverts "a lot," and 31 percent found them very effective. The result – people bought more milk.

Actor Taye Diggs and his son appear in a "got milk?" advert.

How would you advertise this product?

Imagine that you work for an advertising agency. You are asked to create an advert for the robot dog pictured above. You'll begin by considering the communication model. Will the advertisement work best if it is directed to children or to their parents? How will you reach the largest audience? Will a newspaper advert work better than a TV advert? Will you advertise online? These are the kinds of decisions that people in marketing make every day.

Creating a positive feeling

Advertisers don't expect us to rush out to buy their products the minute we see the adverts. They know that advertising messages take time to sink in. Companies want to create positive feelings about their products so that we'll remember them in the future.

Even if we don't pay much attention to an advert, we may remember the **jingle** or music. An advert might make us laugh or smile. If we enjoy the advert, we may feel good about the product. That's the goal. The next time we go shopping and see hundreds of choices, we will probably choose a product we already feel good about.

DID YOU KNOW?

Most watches used in advertisements are set to 10.10. The hands often create a frame around the brand name and form a smiling face.

Advertising techniques

Advertisers use various methods or techniques to create positive feelings toward a product. Carefully planned photographs may make the product look tasty or fun. Advertisers may use facts and figures to prove that one product is better than another. For example, in a car advertisement they may include statistics about how much fuel the car uses per mile, or they may list all the safety features. Advertisers use humour to make us laugh and heart-warming stories to make us feel good about a product.

This advertising campaign for McDonalds was voted "jingle of the century" in 1999. The advert helped McDonald's increase global sales by millions of dollars.

The truth effect

Have you noticed how the same products are advertised over and over again? You begin to learn the jingles. You may even memorize the words of the advert. Advertisers know that when adverts are repeated, they begin to seem true. This is called the "truth effect". Effective jingles, such as the McDonald's jingle, ring true. Who would say that they don't deserve a break? Adverts can draw us to a product through repetition and the appearance of truth.

Seeing is believing

The burger on the top appears in advertisements. It was specially made to look good in photographs. In truth, it probably wouldn't fit into its box. The one on the right looks more like what you'd get at a fast food restaurant. Why is there a difference between the advertised burger and the real burger? Can you trust the things you see in advertisements? How do you know which adverts to believe?

Appeals that work

In addition to creating positive adverts and repeating them, advertisers appeal to people's basic desires and emotions. For example, most people want to be healthy, have fun and avoid embarrassment. The chart below shows some of the most common appeals used in advertisements. Different products require different appeals. Advertisers choose the appeals carefully depending on the product and the audience.

profit	Can the product save you money?
health	Will it make you healthier?
love or romance	Will it increase your chances of finding a boyfriend or girlfriend?
fear	Can this product save you from embarrassment, illness, growing old or looking bad?
admiration	Does someone you admire use this product?
convenience	Will this product or service make your life easier?
fun and pleasure	Is it fun?
vanity	Will it make others admire you?
environmental concern	Does it help the environment?

A closer look

Imagine that an advertising agency is preparing an advert for a new kind of soap. Advertisers might use the **profit** appeal to convince adults that this brand will save them money or the health appeal to report that this soap will kill germs. The advertiser may emphasize that using this soap is fun when advertising on children's TV. The advertiser may use a popular singer (**admiration**) to appeal to teenagers. Advertisers may use more than one appeal in a single advert.

TODAY
Thinking green

TOMORROW
Planning for blue

TOYOTA
toyota.com/future

Can today's environmental thinking inspire tomorrow's technology? Toyota believes so. Since its launch, the Prius has earned the love of millions of forward-thinking drivers. We estimate our hybrid technology has saved a billion gallons of gas and lowered CO_2 emissions by billions of pounds.* It's also paving the way for the next generation of environmental vehicles. Like cars charged at home. Or cars that will run solely on electricity, or consume hydrogen and emit only water. Because when it comes to thinking green, the sky's the limit.

*Estimated savings compares each U.S. hybrid vehicle's EPA combined mpg rating with its segment average based on latest EPA Trends Report (driven 15,000 miles annually). Actual mileage will vary. ©2009

This advertisement appeals to drivers who care about the environment.

Advertising is an important part of the **economy**. Thousands of people are employed in the advertising industry. Many experts believe that advertising helps individuals, the country and the world.

Advertising creates jobs

Advertising helps companies increase sales and leads to higher profits. Higher profits help companies grow. Growing companies buy raw materials, build new factories and purchase other services. They also hire more workers who then have more money to spend. The economy becomes stronger when people have good jobs.

In the past vehicle advertisements used different appeals. What appeal is being used in this advert?

Helping the world economy

Many companies now sell products all over the world. One example is Procter & Gamble (P&G). P&G makes 300 different brands and sells products to almost 5 billion customers in 180 countries. Many of the world's most powerful brands, such as Apple, Microsoft and Coca-Cola, hire workers all over the world. The workers earn money that they spend in their own countries, which helps those economies grow stronger.

Encouraging new product development

Advertising encourages companies to develop new and better products. Companies count on advertisements to draw attention to their new inventions or improvements in older products. Some products fail, of course. But others last forever.

Advertisers will try to turn this new car into a top seller.

Growing business

According to a study in the UK, money spent on advertising helps the economy. This does not mean that every advert increases a company's sales. Some adverts work; others do not. Instead, the study shows that advertising has a positive effect on business.

Presenting choices

Advertising doesn't just introduce new products. It also presents a full range of choices. Adverts may offer additional information about a product. How does it work? What does it cost? What special features does it include? This information helps people make better choices. Advertising encourages people to compare products by considering size, style, price, options and quality.

New parents have many choices to make when buying for their babies.

Making shopping convenient

Today many people are buying products and services online. By looking at company websites and online shops, they can find what they need without leaving home. Experts expect online shopping to increase dramatically in the coming years.

DID YOU KNOW?

British shoppers rank number one in the world in online shopping. Almost two-thirds of British adults shop online. The latest figures available rank Denmark second and Norway third. Australia is sixth, and US shoppers come in fourteenth.

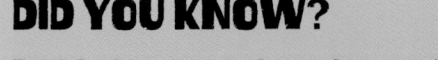

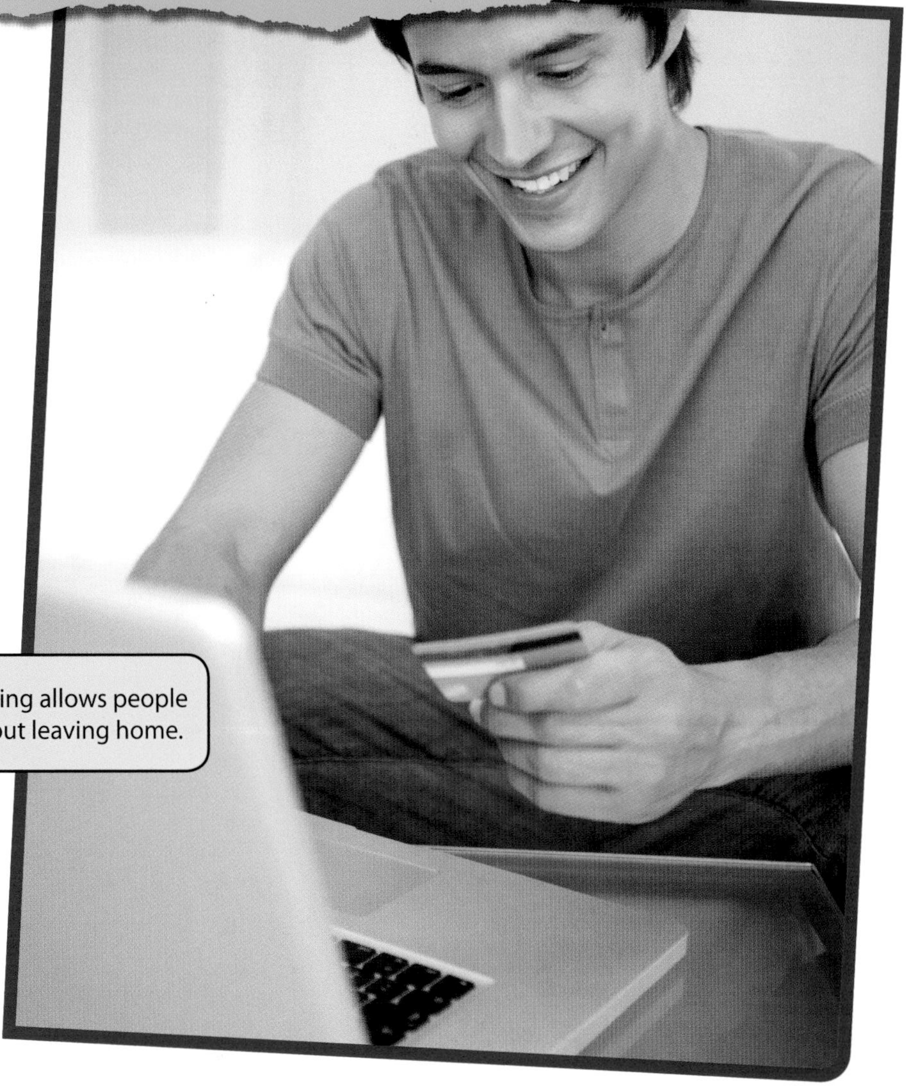

Online shopping allows people to shop without leaving home.

Providing new business opportunities

Online advertising makes it possible for individuals to market their own products. The website Esty provides a place for people to market handmade items. People who make toys, jewellery, clothing, food items and much more can now sell their products online. This is easier and cheaper than opening an ordinary shop.

Advertising lowers prices

In order to sell more, companies may lower prices or offer sales. A well-known study showed that advertising reduces prices even without special sales. That's because the more items a company sells, the less it costs to make each one. This is called **economy of scale**. Companies pass the savings on to customers.

Advertisements alert **consumers** to sales.

Advertisements support important causes

Sometimes businesses include charities in their advertising. In 2012 Marks & Spencer designed a marketing campaign called "shwopping". Their adverts urge shoppers to leave an older item when they buy something new. Marks & Spencer's provides "shwop drops" in its branches. The shop sends the older items to Oxfam, an agency that helps the poor. The items are then given to people in need. These advertising campaigns increase sales and help others. However, some people believe it is better to give money or goods directly to charities.
Many charities and other organizations create their own public service adverts to reach the public. Shops or companies may make it easy to give to charity, but their real goal is to increase their own sales.

Bigger and better?

You can test the idea of economy of scale at the supermarket. Compare the cost of a giant box of cereal to the cost of the smallest box of the same cereal. Which one costs less per serving? Test other products. Does buying more reduce the price per serving? Remember that bigger is not always better – especially if the item might go bad before it is used.

Comparison shopping helps consumers save money.

Advertising supports entertainment

TV networks charge large fees to advertisers. These fees are used to support programming and other TV costs. In 2011 the average price of a 30-second advert on UK TV was about £100,000. Sporting events, such as the 2012 Olympics, depend on the money from TV advertising. Major US TV network NBC sold more than $1 billion worth of adverts to broadcast during the Olympics. The money is divided between the TV network and the Olympic committee.

Newspapers and magazines also depend on advertising money. Without advertising, the newspapers would have to double their prices. Today many newspapers and magazines publish articles online. The adverts appear online as well.

Companies pay a lot of money to show their adverts during popular sporting events.

WHAT DO YOU THINK?

TNS Media Intelligence reports that a typical prime-time TV programme in the United States includes 13 minutes and 52 seconds of adverts and 7 minutes, 59 seconds of product placement appearances. The BBC in the UK and PBS in the United States do not include advertisements. Instead supporters make contributions or pay a license fee. Compare public TV to network programming. Would you be willing to pay fees to watch TV without advertising?

Advertising supports websites

Many websites use adverts to help pay the costs of running the site. Companies pay a fee to the website owner each time someone clicks on their adverts. Sometimes the website owner is an organization, school or individual. Not everyone is pleased about all the adverts on websites. But the adverts can be an important source of money for some organizations.

Some people believe that advertisements are harmful. They point to advertisements that deceive us. Some advertisements are misleading. Common ways advertisers mislead consumers include:

• weasel words that suggest a positive meaning without really making any guarantee that can be measured. Phrases such as "people say", "most people agree", and "studies show" are weasel words.

• the bandwagon technique, which is the suggestion that everyone else is using the product so you should too. Celebrity adverts may also use this technique. Just because a celebrity is using the product does not mean you should.

• glittering generalities that use appealing words and images to sell the product. For example, the product will "change your life" or turn you into a "cool dude". Again, this cannot be proved.

Making false claims or lying in adverts is illegal. Companies cannot say that a medicine cures an illness unless there is scientific proof that it does so. However, misleading advertisements are not illegal. It is up to consumers to read or watch adverts closely and make their own judgements.

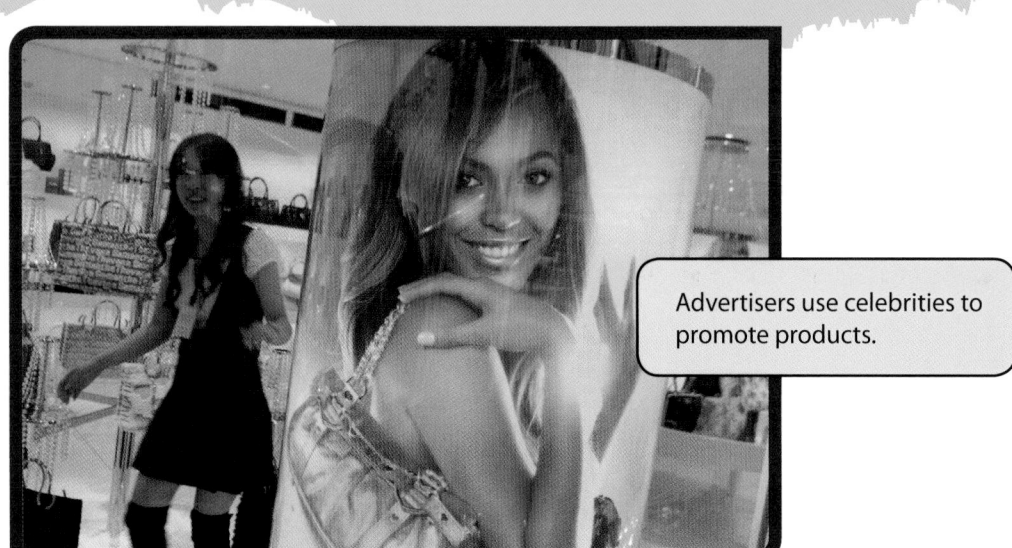

Advertisers use celebrities to promote products.

Be advert aware

A chocolate shop in the local shopping precinct posts a big sign in the window that says "World's Best Chocolates". Are they really the best in the world? There is no way to prove or disprove the claim. This kind of advertising is called puffery. It is not against the law. The shop is stating an opinion, not trying to deceive customers.

Shops or restaurants may advertise that they offer the "world's best".

Advertising causes us to want more

Advertising creates a demand for more and better things. "New and improved" are words often used in adverts. This leads us to think that what we now have is not good enough. Advertising may convince people that the things they want are actually things that they need. For some people, shopping becomes a habit that has little to do with their basic needs. Advertisements convince them to buy more. Studies show that unhappy adults believe that owning more things will make them happier. They buy things but still feel unhappy. So they buy even more. It can become a never-ending cycle.

Advertising may lead us to buy things we don't need and can't afford.

Advertising leads to overspending

Advertising may lead some people to overspend. Items on sale seem too good to miss. Some shoppers get so excited that they buy more than they can afford and more than they need. Some sales advertise "buy two get one free". It may be a good deal. But if you only need one, why buy two? Consumers should think carefully before they buy.

Many people today use credit cards. This habit makes it easy to overspend. The result is that millions of people are in debt. They owe more money than they have. Advertising, especially by credit card companies, makes it easy to spend money. Unfortunately, it's not so easy to get out of debt.

WHAT DO YOU THINK?

Children's writer Maurice Sendak once said, "There must be more to life than having everything!" What things are more important than material goods?

Landfills are full of electronics that still work but are not the latest technology. Throwing away too much is harmful to the environment.

Advertising leads to waste

If advertising leads to overspending, then it also leads to waste. We've become a throwaway society. We replace old but still usable objects with brand new ones. We toss the old ones away. This practice is not just wasteful. It's also dangerous. Plastics, electronic equipment and other waste products release dangerous chemicals that may cause illnesses. Advertising may be partly to blame for the piles of refuse in the world's landfills.

Adverts are annoying

Many people think adverts are annoying. In a recent survey, 91 percent of Americans reported being annoyed by adverts. As many as 43 percent said they would ignore any company that sent them two or more online adverts or **spam** emails. Even so, the adverts may influence what they buy. Of course, people can turn off the TV or stop buying newspapers and magazines. But some adverts are unavoidable. Ambient adverts surround us. Online adverts appear with every click of the mouse.

How Consumers Feel About Advertising

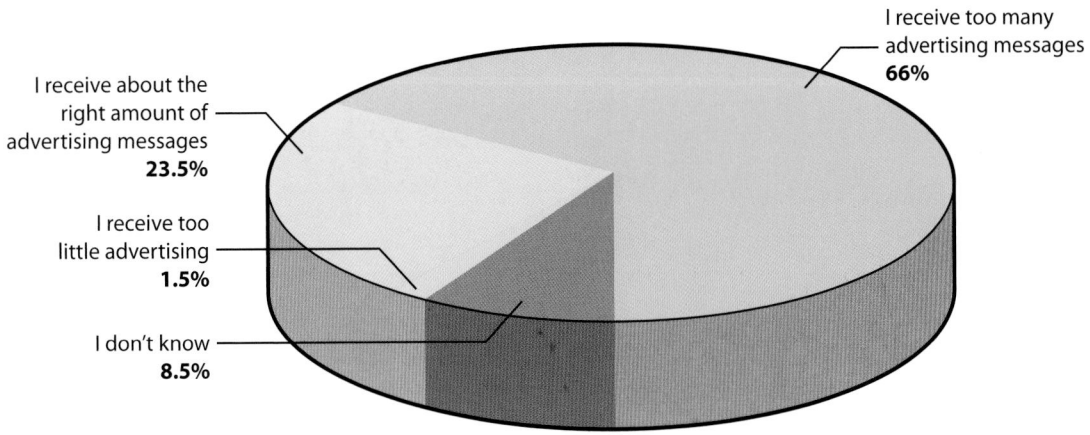

I receive too many advertising messages
66%

I receive about the right amount of advertising messages
23.5%

I receive too little advertising
1.5%

I don't know
8.5%

A 2012 survey asked people in the UK and the United States how they felt about the amount of advertising they received via email, text messages, websites and other digital sources.

Advertising to children

Many advertisers target children. They not only sell items that appeal to children, but they know that children influence what their parents buy. Children up to the age of 11 spend more than £18.6 billion of their own money each year. Teenagers (aged 12 to 19) spend more than £523 billion. Some reports suggest that children and teenagers have a big influence on their parents' spending each year. Considering this huge amount of money, it is not surprising that advertising aimed at children is increasing. Today advertisers spend more than £10 billion per year advertising to children and teens.

Many adverts aimed at children suggest that certain products will turn them into cool, popular kids.

Surrounded by adverts

Children and young people have greater access to TV and computers today than in the past. In the UK about 70 percent of children aged 8 to 18 have a TV in their bedrooms. This means that they are watching TV without their parents' supervision. Children are online, playing video games and using mobile phones. In some parts of the world, advertisers even buy space at schools, putting adverts on gym floors, in buses or in hallways.

WHAT DO YOU THINK?

Advertisers studied nagging and discovered that children aged 12 to 17 usually ask parents for a product about nine times before the parents give in. Many adverts directed at children and teenagers encourage them to nag their parents to buy particular products. Do you think decisions based on nagging are good decisions? Why or why not? If not, who is to blame – parents for giving in, children for nagging or advertisers for encouraging nagging?

Programme or advert?

Studies show that children under the age of 8 cannot tell the difference between an advertisement and a TV programme. They are not able to make good judgements. Older children know the difference between nutritious food and junk food, but younger children do not. If an advert claims that sugary cereals are healthy, young children believe it – especially if a favourite TV or cartoon character says it is true.

Party, game or advert?

Advertisers know the power of word-of-mouth advertising, so they sometimes use children to advertise products to other children. This is called peer-to-peer marketing. For example, a company may sponsor a children's party. The host child invites friends to come and try a new product such as nail polish or sports equipment. It may feel like an ordinary party, but it is really advertising.

Events and contests may be hidden advertisements too. A shop may hold a special event with games and activities to encourage children to buy a certain brand of sports equipment. Restaurants may give out vouchers as prizes for school contests. This kind of hidden advertising occurs online too. Companies sponsor activities, games and contests that include adverts and use product placement.

WHAT DO YOU THINK?

Sweden and Norway forbid advertising aimed at children younger than the age of 12. Denmark and Belgium limit advertising to children. Do you agree with them? Should the government ban advertising to children?

Some people believe that advertising should not be allowed on children's TV programmes.

The future of advertising

Advertising keeps changing to reflect how people shop and communicate. Online advertising is increasing rapidly. Advertisers will find ways to make ads more fun and less annoying. For example, future online and mobile phone adverts may flash across screens and disappear.

Viral advertising

Advertisers will increase peer-to-peer marketing. Viral adverts are a form of peer-to-peer marketing. Companies create funny videos and use celebrities to sell their products. These short video adverts may spread like a virus when people forward them to friends. When that happens, they are called viral videos. Recently Samsung Corporation hired Jay-Z and Usher to make short video adverts. The videos reached millions of viewers because people sent them to friends.

How Much Countries Spend on Online Advertising
(in billions)

Country	2011	2012	2013 (est.)	2014 (est.)
United States	32.0	39.5	46.5	52.8
Japan	7.21	8.10	9.58	10.17
United Kingdom	7.13	7.91	8.70	9.70
Germany	5.16	6.59	7.42	8.62
China	4.57	6.21	7.63	9.46
France	2.88	3.20	3.50	3.95
Canada	2.16	2.54	2.86	3.23
Italy	1.52	1.78	2.01	2.27
Spain	1.20	1.41	1.48	1.67

Targeted adverts

Shops target individual consumers by providing them with loyalty cards to use when paying for their goods. These cards track what shoppers buy. Shoppers may get vouchers or email adverts for these products. This kind of targeted advertising is sure to increase, especially online.

Reaching new populations

Online advertising, mobile phone apps and product placement is not limited by geography. Advertisers will reach out to new consumers around the world. Advertisers are particularly targeting Chinese consumers. China has a huge population and a growing economy. Some adverts, like the one below, are not even limited to people on Earth!

This giant advertisement can be seen from space.

WHAT DO YOU THINK?

Do you think it is appropriate for companies to track the websites you visit? Why or why not?

Are you ready to debate some of these issues with your friends?
If so, these five tips may help.

1. Be prepared. Do some research before you begin. Make a list of points you plan to debate. Then think of arguments on the other side. Then you'll be prepared when your friend mentions them.

2. State your opinions clearly. It's useful to provide examples and statistics.

3. Listen carefully. After all, you cannot respond effectively unless you understand exactly what your friend is saying. You can ask your friend to repeat the comment or provide further information.

4. Keep your cool. In a good debate there is no clear winner or loser. You will win some points and lose others. You may even find that some of your friend's comments make sense. That's not bad. It shows that you are keeping an open mind.

5. Have fun! Debate is a great way to explore the issues.

admiration act of liking and respecting something or someone

advertising campaign series of advertising messages that share a single idea or theme

ambient advert advert placed in an unsual place or on an unusual item

brand name that identifies a product

capitalism economic and political system in which private owners control a country's trade and industry

charity organization that provides help or raises money for those in need

consumer person who buys things

digital device electronic device, such as a mobile phone

economy wealth or resources of a country or region

economy of scale savings in the cost of producing goods due to an increase in the number of items produced

jingle short verse or song with catchy repetition

logo symbol that represents a company or brand that is designed to be easily recognizable

profit financial gain

spam electronic junk mail

targeted advert advert aimed at a specific audience

Find out more

Books

Advertisements (Getting the Message), Sean Connolly (Franklin Watts, 2009)

Advertising (Ethical Debates), Jen Green (Wayland, 2011)

Advertising Attack (Mastering Media), Laura Hensley (Raintree, 2011)

Big Fat Lies: Advertising Tricks (Slim Goodbody's Lighten Up!), John Burstein and
Slim Goodbody (San Val, 2008)

Websites

The Advertising Standards Authority (ASA)
http://www.asa.org.uk
The Advertising Standards Authority acts as a "watchdog" that regulates advertising
in the UK across all media. Visit their website to find out more about the work they do
to protect the public against misleading, harmful or offensive advertisements.

"Duke University Libraries: Ad* Access"
library.duke.edu/digitalcollections/adaccess/
Check out this US website to see a fascinating collection of American advertisements
dating from 1911 to 1955.

Places to visit

The Museum of Brands, Packaging, and Advertising
2 Colville Mews, Lonsdale Road
London W11 2LR
http://www.museumofbrands.com
This small museum houses a unique collection of vintage British advertising
and product branding dating back more than 150 years.

Further research

- Keep a record of advertising for one 24-hour period. Write down how many adverts you see, where you see them and what appeals they use to get your attention. Share this with your family and friends.

- Develop an advertising campaign for a cause in which you believe. Choose a target audience, the type of media you will use and the appeals that will work best to promote your cause.

- Research one product. How much money does the company spend on advertising each year? Where do they advertise? What kinds of appeals do they use? Do you think the adverts are effective? Why or why not?

Index